So Glad we're Sisters

by
Marianne Richmond

To

From

Date

I'm so glad
we're sisters!

I feel like I have a
"built-in" best friend
for life.

To say we go "way back" pretty
much sums it up.
From sharing the TV, bathroom
and clothing...
To negotiating chores...

and "co-experiencing" family dinners, vacations and chaos.

For as long as I can remember... you were there.

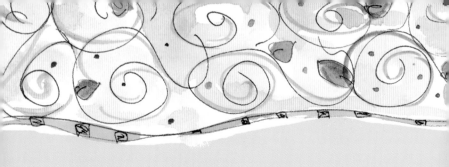

Oh... we've had some pretty good
fights, haven't we?

Sometimes I wasn't sure we'd
ever forgive each other.

But we always did.

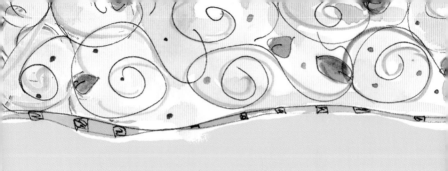

Until the
next blow
out.

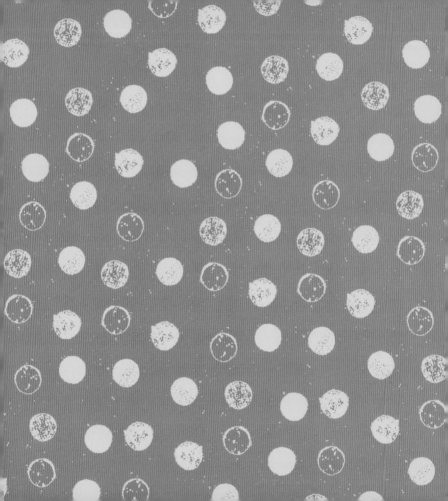

I love how
our relationship
grows and
changes
with time.

Thank you for all the ways

you've been there for me...

playmate, teacher,

confidante, cheerleader,

and friend.

Publicist,

therapist and

defense attorney,

too.

I know my feelings
are safe with you.

I admire you.

Your spirit,
strength and
wisdom.

Your crazy

sense of humor.

Sometimes
I wish I could be
more like you...

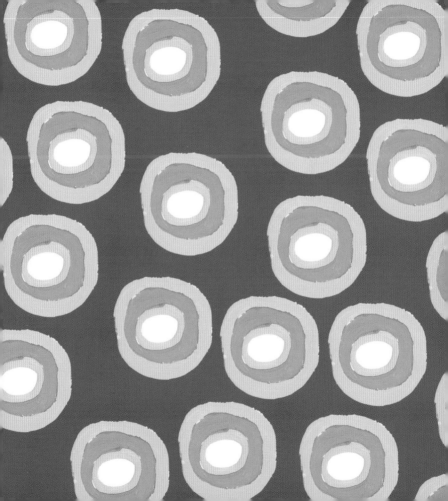

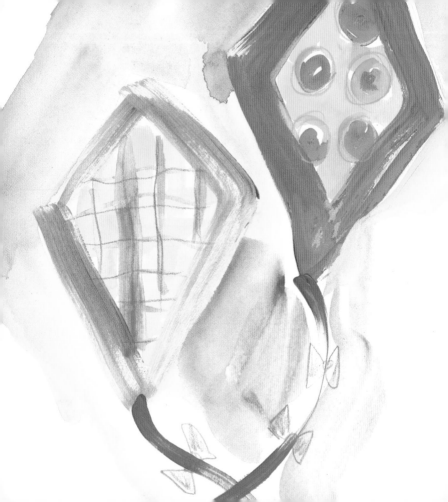

But then I'd miss out on cherishing you for who you are.

And how my life is enriched because of you.

I
love
that we're
connected.

Thanks for listening
to me gripe.

And for loving me
through any mood.

I appreciate your advice.

Even though I
occasionally
tell you otherwise.

Thanks, sis, for making me laugh... sometimes so hard I thought I'd bust.

I love that you
usually know
what I'm
thinking.

It's like we have this secret connection that's ours alone.

You know me like
no other.

People will come
and go in life.

They will be there for
a reason or a season.

But sisters are forever.

I'm
so *glad*
you're
mine.

So Glad we're Sisters

Marianne Richmond Studios, Inc.
3900 Stinson Boulevard NE
Minneapolis, MN 55421
www.mariannerichmond.com

ISBN 10: 0-9763101-4-7
ISBN 13: 978- 0-9763101-4-3

Illustrations by Marianne Richmond

Book design by Sara Dare Biscan

Printed in China
Second Printing
September 2009

Also available from author & illustrator
Marianne Richmond:

The Gift of an Angel
The Gift of a Memory
Hooray for You!
The Gifts of Being Grand
I Love You So...
Dear Daughter
Dear Son
Dear Granddaughter
Dear Grandson
Dear Mom
My Shoes Take Me Where I Want to Go
Fish Kisses and Gorilla Hugs
I Love You so Much...
Happy Birthday to You!
I Wished for You, an adoption story
You are my Wish come True

To learn more about Marianne's products,
please visit
www.mariannerichmond.com